SPECTRUM®
EARLY YEARS

Basic Beginnings
COUNTING & SEQUENCING

Published by Spectrum®
an imprint of Carson-Dellosa Publishing LLC
Greensboro, NC

Spectrum
An imprint of Carson-Dellosa Publishing, LLC
P.O. Box 35665
Greensboro, NC 27425-5665

carsondellosa.com

ISBN 978-1-60996-887-8   01-044127784

Table of Contents

Welcome to *Basic Beginnings*

Basic Beginnings is a creative and developmentally appropriate series designed to fuel your child's learning potential. The early years of your child's life are bursting with cognitive and physical development. Therefore, it is essential to prepare your child for the basic skills and fine motor skills that are emphasized in the 21ˢᵗ century classroom. Basic skills include concepts such as recognizing letters, numbers, colors, shapes, and identifying same, different, and sequences of events. Fine motor skills are movements produced by small muscles or muscle groups, such as the precise hand movements required to write, cut, glue, and color. A child in preschool spends a lot of his or her day developing these muscles.

Basic Beginnings approaches learning through a developmentally appropriate process—ensuring your child is building the best foundation possible for preschool. Each activity is unique and fun, and stimulates your child's fine motor skills, hand-eye coordination, and ability to follow directions. Help your child complete the activities in this book. Each activity includes simple, step-by-step instructions. Provide your child with pencils, crayons, scissors, and glue for the various and creative activities he or she is about to discover.

Each book also includes three cutout mini books that reinforce the concepts your child is learning. You and your child will enjoy reading these simple stories together. Your child can make each story his or her own by coloring it, cutting it out, and, with your help, stapling the story together. Allow him or her to share the stories with you and others. Your child will begin to recognize sight words, hear vowel sounds, and understand sequences of events as he or she shares these delightful stories. With *Basic Beginnings*, the learning is never confined to the pages!

Counting to 3

Directions: Count the ponies. Color the ponies.

Directions: Trace and write.

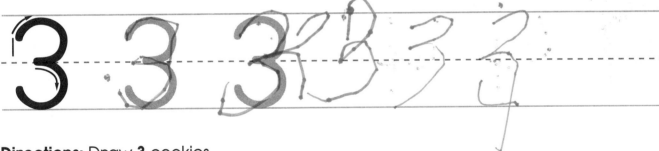

Directions: Draw **3** cookies.

Counting & Sequencing

Counting to 4

Directions: Count the turtles. Crawl like a turtle in **4** circles.

Directions: Trace and write.

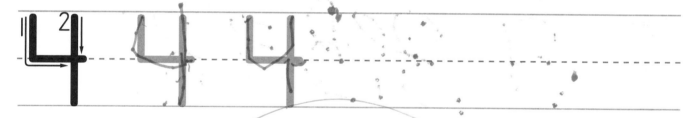

Directions: Draw and color **4** happy faces.

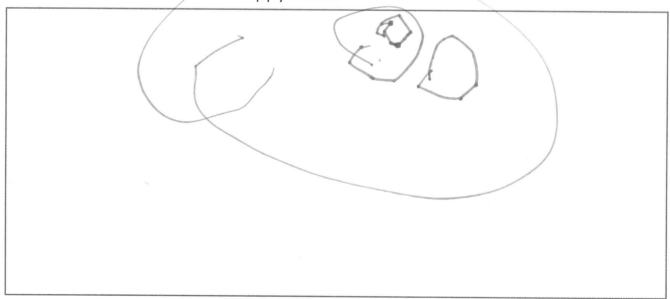

Counting & Sequencing

Counting to 5

Directions: Count the birds. Color the birds blue.

Directions: Trace and write.

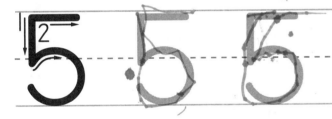

Directions: Draw **5** kites. Then, color.

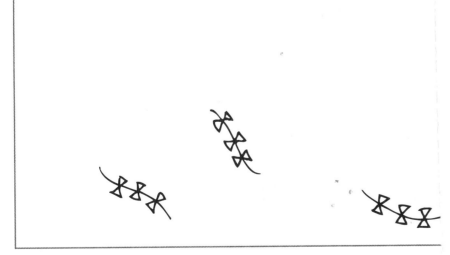

Counting & Sequencing

Counting to 6

Directions: Count the bunnies. Draw a carrot for each bunny.

Directions: Trace and write.

Directions: Connect the dots. Then, color.

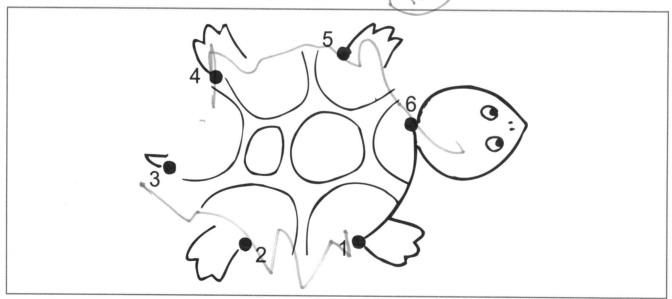

Counting & Sequencing

2

Six silly seals
sat in the sun.

4

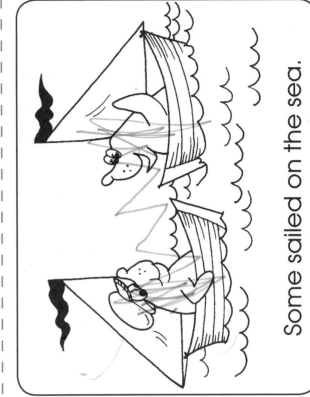

Some sailed on the sea.

1

Six Silly Seals

3

Six silly seals said,
"Let's have fun."

5

Some sat and sang.

Notes to Parents

Directions: First, ask your child to color the mini book. Then, help him or her cut along the dotted lines. Next, have your child arrange the pages in the correct order. Staple the pages together. Read the story out loud to your child.

Extension ideas:

1. Ask your child to tell you what comes first in the story: Six silly seals sat in the sun or some played in the sand.
2. Have your child count the seals on each page. Have him or her jump up and down that many times.
3. Sing a silly song about the number six.
4. Make six seals with play dough.
5. Ask your child to tell a story about his or her favorite number.

8

5

Some played in the sand.

Some played in the band.

7

Counting & Sequencing

Counting to 7

Directions: Count the frogs. Color the frogs.

Directions: Trace and write.

Directions: Draw **7** flowers.

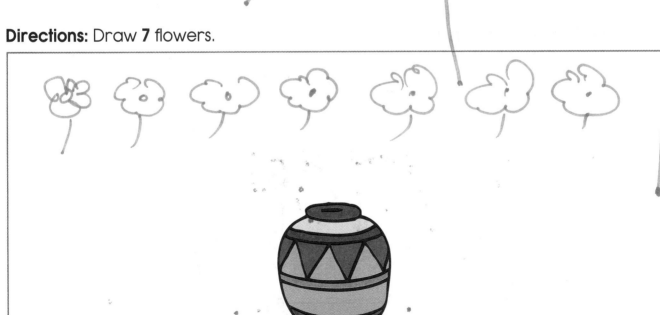

Counting & Sequencing

Counting to 8

Directions: Count the airplanes. Pretend to fly like an airplane for **8** seconds.

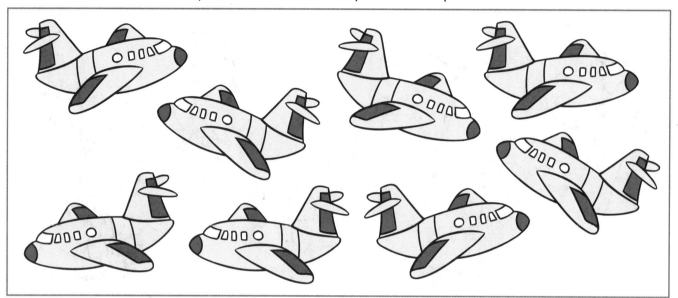

Directions: Trace and write.

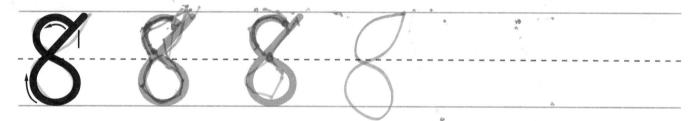

Directions: Connect the dots. Color the sign **red**.

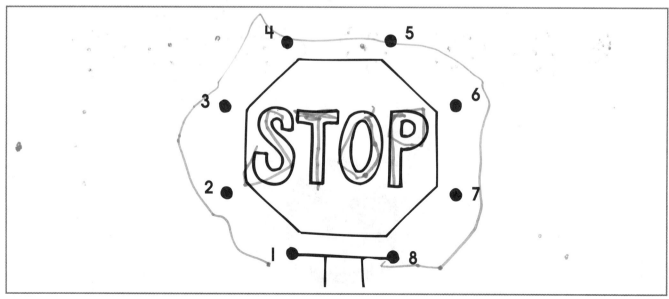

Counting & Sequencing

Counting to 9

Directions: Count the ladybugs. Color each ladybug.

Directions: Trace and write.

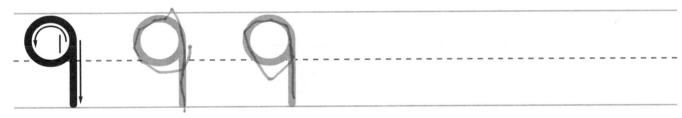

Directions: Draw 9 raindrops.

Counting & Sequencing

Review 0 to 9

Directions: Connect the dots in order. Then, color the rest of the picture.

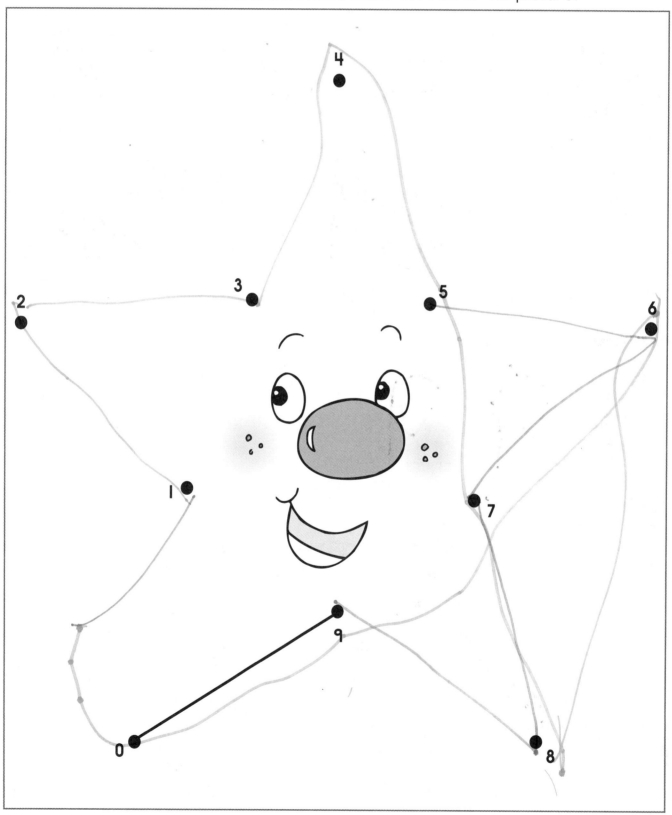

Counting to 10

Directions: Count the fish. Draw bubbles for each fish.

Directions: Trace and write.

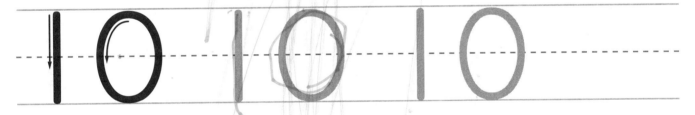

Directions: Draw **10** pennies.

Counting & Sequencing

Counting to 11

Directions: Count the bees. Buzz like a bee for 11 seconds.

Directions: Trace and write.

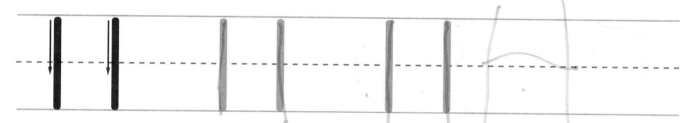

Directions: Draw and color 11 jellybeans.

Counting to 12

Directions: Count the faces. Color the faces.

Directions: Trace and write.

1 2 | 2 | 2

Directions: Connect the dots. Color the wagon **red**.

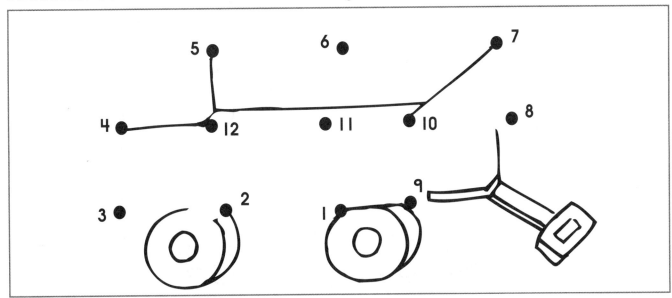

Counting & Sequencing

Counting to 13

Directions: Count the snowmen. Draw a scarf for each snowman.

Directions: Trace and write.

13 13 13

Directions: Draw and color **13** fish in the bowl.

Counting & Sequencing

Counting to 14

Directions: Count the apples. Color the apples **red**.

Directions: Trace and write.

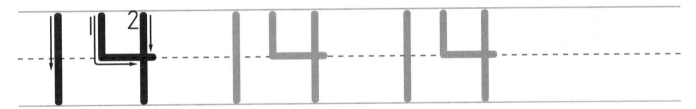

Directions: Draw **14** apples on the tree.

Counting & Sequencing

Counting to 15

Directions: Count the flowers. How many different colors can you count?

Directions: Trace and write.

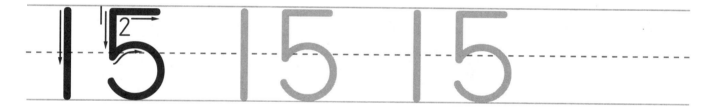

Directions: Draw **15** marbles in the jar.

Counting & Sequencing

Counting to 16

Directions: Count the baseballs. Throw a ball to a friend **16** times.

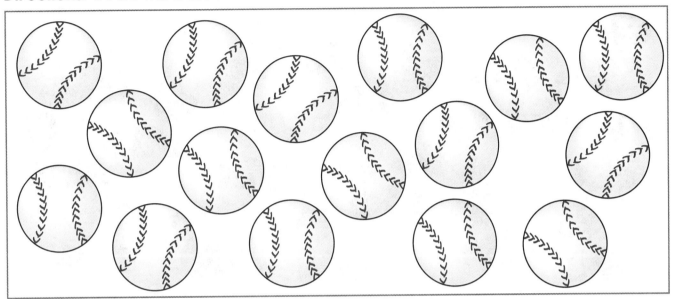

Directions: Trace and write.

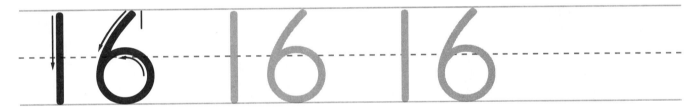

Directions: Draw **16** buttons on the hat. Then, color.

Counting & Sequencing

Counting to 17

Directions: Count the snakes. Slither like a snake for **17** seconds.

Directions: Trace and write.

1 7   1 7   1 7

Directions: Draw **17** polka dots on the shirt. Then, color.

Counting to 18

Directions: Count the balloons. How many different colors can you count?

Directions: Trace and write.

Directions: Draw **18** spots on the dog.

Counting & Sequencing

Counting to 19

Directions: Count the balls. Color the balls.

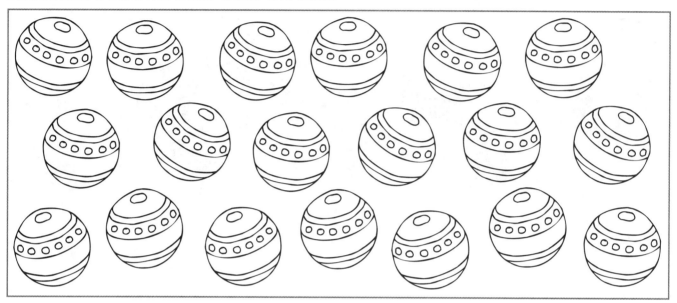

Directions: Trace and write.

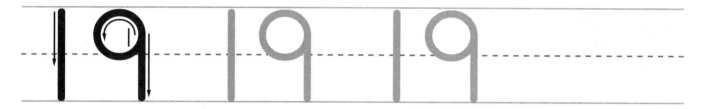

Directions: Draw 19 eggs in the basket. Then, color.

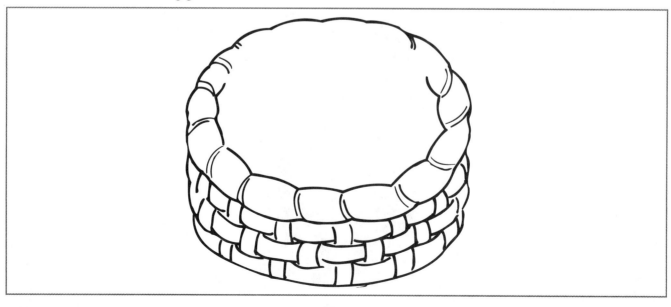

Counting to 20

Directions: Count the chicks. Cheep like a chick **20** times.

Directions: Trace and write.

20 20 20

Directions: Draw **20 black** spots on the ladybug. Then, color it **red**.

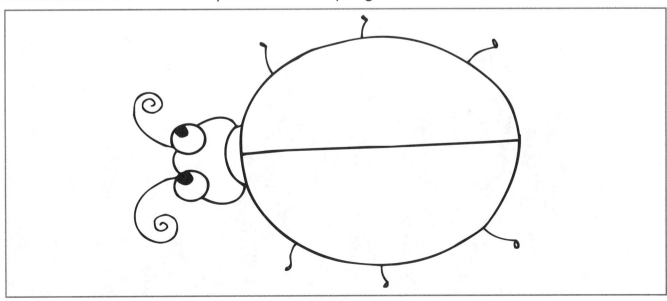

Counting & Sequencing

Review 1 to 20

Directions: Connect the dots. Color the picture.

Counting & Sequencing

2

One little bike . . . .

4

Two little dolls . . . .

1

One, Two, Three!

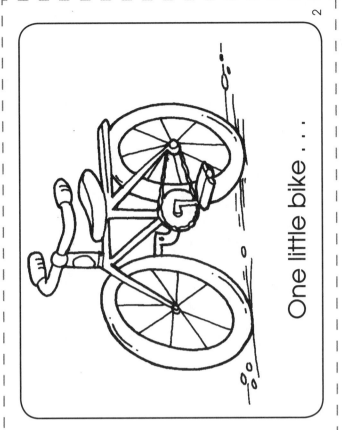

3

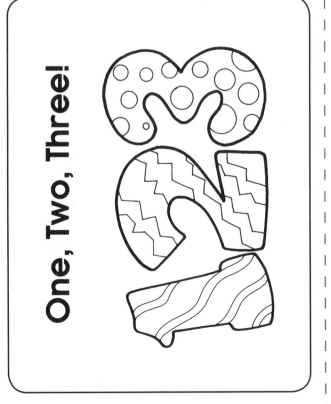

and one little boy.

33

Counting & Sequencing

6

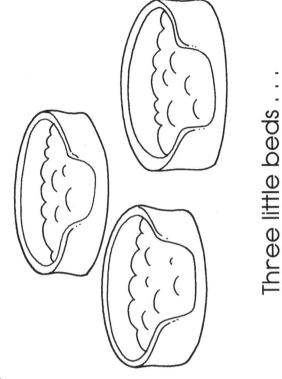

Three little beds . . . .

8

Notes to Parents

Directions: First, ask your child to color the mini book. Then, help him or her cut along the dotted lines. Next, have your child arrange the pages in the correct order. Staple the pages together. Read the story out loud to your child.

Extension ideas:

1. Ask your child to find **1** toy he or she loves.
2. Have your child count the cats on page 7. Name the cats.
3. Make up a rhyme about counting to **3**.
4. Ask your child what comes first in the story: two little dolls or three little kittens.
5. Ask your child to use his or her fingers to show **1**, **2**, and **3**.

5

and two little girls.

7

and three little kittens.

Count the Dots!

Directions: Color the seal! Count the dots in each section. Use the color key to find the correct color for each section.

KEY

●	●●	●●●	●●●●
blue	yellow	red	green

●●●●●	●●●●●●	●●●●●●●
orange	purple	black

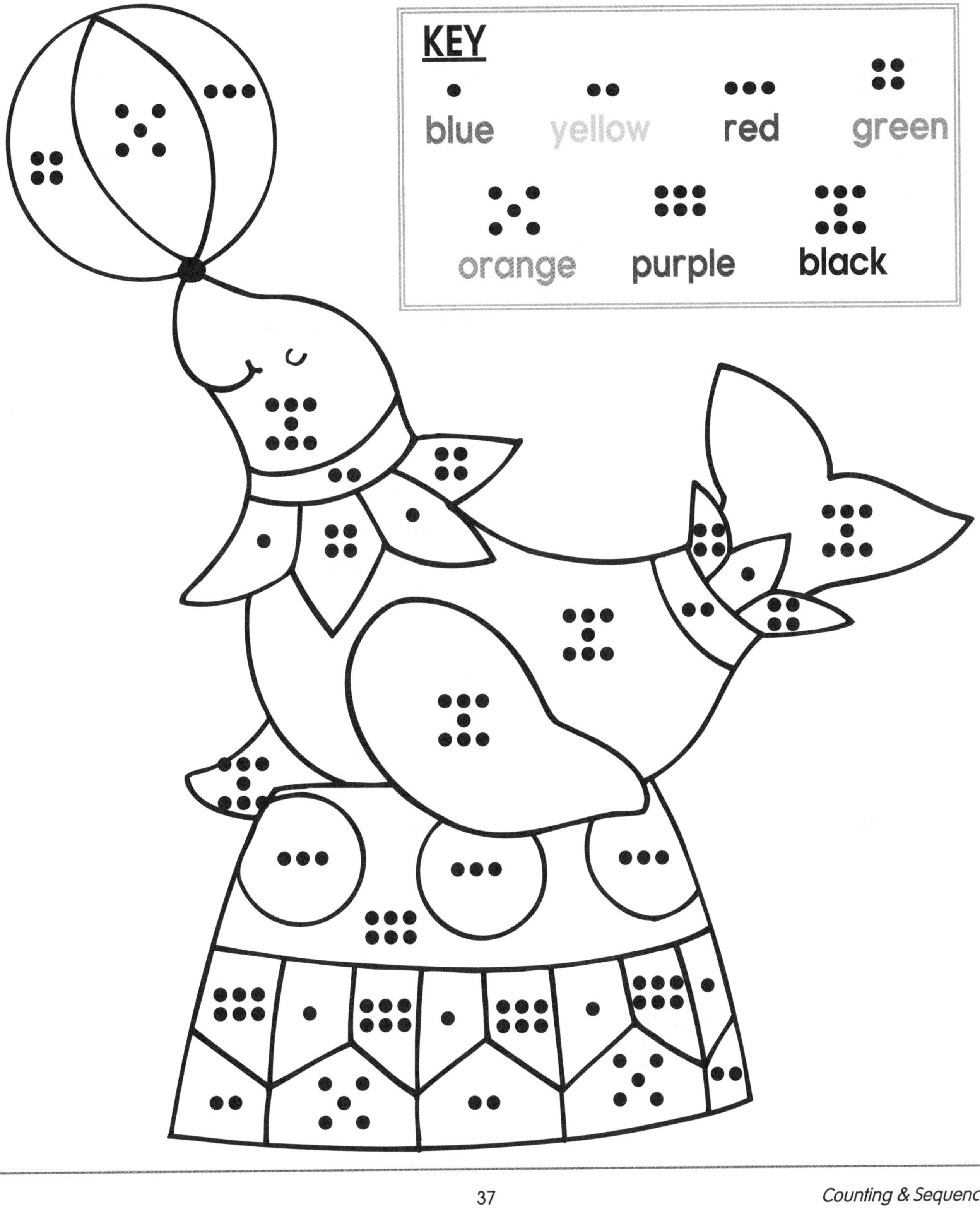

Sequencing Numbers

Directions: Fill in the missing numbers.

1 _ _ _ _ _ 3 _ _ _ _ _ 5

_ _ _ _ _ 7 _ _ _ _ _ 9 _ _ _ _ _

11 _ _ _ _ _ 13 _ _ _ _ _

15 _ _ _ _ _ 17 _ _ _ _ _

19 _ _ _ _ _

Counting & Sequencing

Sequencing Puzzle: Flamingo

Directions: Cut along the dashed lines. Glue each piece in the correct order. Color the flamingo.

39

Counting & Sequencing

Sequencing Puzzle: Penguin

Directions: Cut along the dashed lines. Glue each piece in the correct order. Color the penguin.

Bead Patterns

Directions: Look at the beads. Color the bead that should come next.

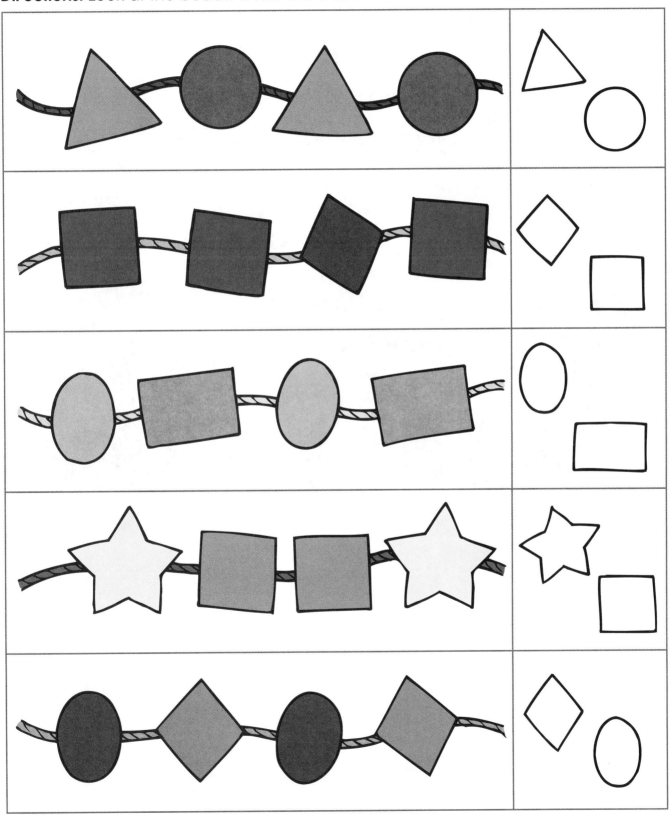

Counting & Sequencing

Sequencing: Slide

Directions: Look at the pictures. Follow the directions below.

Write a **1** under the picture that happened **first**.
Write a **2** under the picture that happened **next**.
Write a **3** under the picture that happened **last**.

Counting & Sequencing

Largest to Smallest Kids

Directions: Color the kids below. Cut them out. Glue them in the correct order, from largest to smallest.

Largest	**Smallest**

Counting & Sequencing

Smallest to Largest Teddy Bears

Directions: Color the bears below. Cut them out. Glue them in the correct order, from smallest to largest.

Smallest   **Largest**

47   *Counting & Sequencing*

2

Two turtles at play.

1

Two Turtles

4

They play with a top.

3

They have tons of toys.

6

They watch TV.

8

Notes to Parents

Directions: First, ask your child to color the mini book. Then, help him or her cut along the dotted lines. Next, have your child arrange the pages in the correct order. Staple the pages together. Read the story out loud to your child.

Extension ideas:
1. Ask your child to draw what the two turtles will do next.
2. Have your child count the turtles on each page. Ask your child to turn every time he or she counts a turtle.
3. Grab and decorate two paper plates to make a tambourine. Place the two plates together, put beans or rice inside, and tape together. Add streamers for extra fun.

5

They play with a toy lion.

7

Two tired turtles are sleeping in a tent.

Sequencing: Good Morning

Directions: Read the story below. Color it. Write **1**, **2**, and **3** to show the correct order of the story.

Sara woke up and stretched. She got out of bed and put on her clothes. After she was dressed, she ate her breakfast.

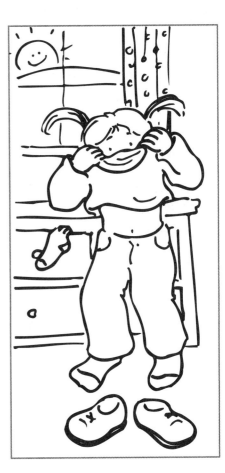

Sequencing Story: Busy Boy!

Directions: Color and cut out the story cards on page 55. Read the story below. Glue the cards in the correct order.

Juan was a busy boy! Juan began the day roller skating. After he was done skating he was hungry, so he ate an ice cream cone. Juan ended the day playing with his cars.

First   **Next**   **Last**

Counting & Sequencing

Sequencing Story: Busy Boy!

Directions: Color and cut out the story cards below. Glue the cards in the correct order on page 54.

Counting & Sequencing

Sequencing: Baby Chick

Directions: Look at the pictures. Follow the directions below.

Write a **1** under the picture that happened **first**.
Write a **2** under the picture that happened **next**.
Write a **3** under the picture that happened **last**.

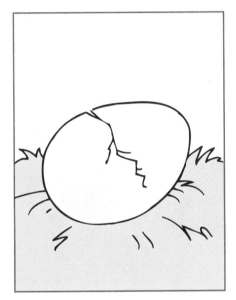  

Counting & Sequencing

Sequencing Rhyme: A Mouse!

Directions: Color and cut out the story cards on page 59. Read the rhyme below. Glue the cards in the correct order.

A mouse ran out of the house. He went to find cheese. The cheese made him sneeze.

1	2	3

Counting & Sequencing

Sequencing Rhyme: A Mouse!

Directions: Color and cut out the story cards below. Glue the cards in the correct order on page 58.

Sequencing: Lollipop

Directions: Look at the pictures. Follow the directions below.

Write a **1** under the picture that happened **first**.
Write a **2** under the picture that happened **next**.
Write a **3** under the picture that happened **last**.

Counting & Sequencing

Sequencing Story: The Three Wishes

Directions: Color and cut out the story cards on page 63. Read the story below.
Glue the cards in the correct order on a separate sheet of paper.

Once upon a time, there was a little boy. He lost three of his teeth all at once. He did not want money from the tooth fairy—he wanted a wish for each tooth he lost. The tooth fairy arrived and said she would be happy to grant him three wishes.

For his first wish, he asked for a pony. He always wanted a pony. Unfortunately, the little boy discovered that he did not know how to ride it. As soon as he climbed on the pony's back, it threw him off!

The little boy's second wish was for a new bike. The tooth fairy granted his wish and gave him a big new bike. Unfortunately, the bike was too big for the little boy. When he got on the bike, he fell over and skinned his elbow.

Finally, it was time for his third wish. The little boy said, "My third wish is not to have any more wishes. No more ponies, no more bikes, no more wishes!" The tooth fairy flew away, but she left three dollars under the little boy's pillow!

Directions: What is one thing you would wish for? Draw it.

Sequencing Story: The Three Wishes

Directions: Color and cut out the story cards below. Glue the cards in the correct order on a separate sheet of paper. Share the story with a friend!

Counting & Sequencing